Life with Mikey
Learning Disability

Written & Created
By

Michael J. Falcaro

If you have a learning disability, you may be trying to understand your differences. Maybe understanding a little about what Mikey went through would be helpful. Mikey has had a difficult time learning in regular classrooms because he didn't learn the same way as his classmates because he has a learning disability. When someone has a learning disability it does not mean they are dumb, unmotivated, or lazy. We all process information differently, but some of us have unique ways of learning. Most classes are taught in a particular way that works for the majority of students, but not everyone learns the same way. We are all wired differently and struggle in classes when we are expected to learn the same way as our classmates.

At a very young age, Mikey noticed he couldn't keep up with others. He struggled with listening to the teacher, being expected to memorize facts for upcoming tests, writing down what was on the board before the teacher erased it, reading as fast as others, and having a time limit to do work and tests. So much frustration followed Mikey throughout school.

In each class, Mikey felt the same. Everyone was expected to learn in the same way and to fit the mold of the class as a whole. The more Mikey would try to keep up, the more behind he would get. He would lose his place and have to stop the class to ask what page they were on.

He needed more time to write things down or take a quiz. The more he struggled, the more his classmates noticed his differences.

Some classmates were mean and called him names while others felt sorry for him, which made him sad and uncomfortable. The struggles he was having academically followed him socially from the classroom to the playground.

Kids can be cruel, especially when they don't understand how their actions or words impact someone else's feelings. Words can be powerful. Even though we shouldn't care what people say, after a while, between the mean kids and the disappointment from teachers, Mikey began to think poorly of himself. For the longest time, Mikey believed there was something wrong with him.

Mikey began to give up on himself and start thinking he was stupid and would never reach his goals. Eventually, teachers suggested he should be tested to find out why Mikey struggled. He dreaded tests since they were one of the areas that he struggled with. At the time, Mikey didn't understand why teachers wanted to him to take tests that would label him, but he soon found out the tests were to help figure out how he learned differently than others. There are many different learning disabilities including Non-verbal Learning, Oral and Written Language Comprehension Disorder, Auditory Disorder, Visual Disorder, ADHD, Dyscalculia, Dysgraphia, Dyslexia and all Mikey heard was a bunch of big words that started with the letter "D" and thought of himself as a Disorder.

The reason for the tests and labels is to identify the different ways Mikey learns so that teachers and caregivers can understand how to best help him. By taking all of the tests, it actually helped the adults identify how we learn differently so they can understand how we learn. Mikey was scared of getting help, because he didn't want to be judged. Having a learning disability simply identifies how you process information differently; which will help you learn to the best of your ability.

Mikey went from feeling helpless and hopeless to getting help and having hope. Letting adults help him along the way takes courage. All kids learn differently, we just have to use our heads to recognize that allowing others to help isn't a weakness but rather a strength. Learning about ourselves and how we learn will help us all throughout life.

Mikey learned that he has Auditory Disorder, Dyslexia and ADHD. Now that adults were aware of how he learned, instead of expecting him to learn the way they usually taught, they began to teach the way he learned. It took a long time for Mikey to warm up to having learning disabilities and reminded himself that they were just alternative ways of learning.

By acknowledging his different style of learning, he began to do better in the classrooms. Instead of giving up, he would raise his hand and try. He sometimes wore headphones to listen to books and had teachers read him his tests. By using different methods to get the information into his brain, he began to learn so much better.

His confidence began to rise and the more aware he became of how he needed to learn, the more empowered he became knowing that he wasn't dumb or stupid, but simply learned differently.

Having a disability of any kind doesn't make you less than anyone else. Differences should be proudly embraced and accepted.

Being different may make some people uncomfortable because they don't understand. People often act out in a negative way to what's different. No matter how different we all are, what matters is that we accept ourselves, especially our differences.

Haters are going to hate. You should never allow someone to control you or change your way of thinking about something, someone, or yourself. You are in control of your actions, thoughts and future. The more you accept yourself, the more others will do the same. Friendships are diverse and different, just like the way we learn.

Haters Gonna Hate

Friendships are diverse, just like learning

Mikey realized that he had to be comfortable with who he is and his differences. Mike began to have his classroom success follow him onto the playground and began to do better academically and socially, all because he knew his differences didn't disable him. A disability does not mean inability, it just means your abilities are different than others.

Before you care about anyone else in life, you have to care about yourself. Love who you are, because you are special. Just like Mikey, you are unique and no one else in the world is exactly like you.

Self Love

Having a learning disability is nothing to be ashamed of or sad about. Mikey felt lost for the longest time because he felt he needed to be fixed; but he found himself when he realized he was never broken to begin with. Understanding how he learns differently helped Mikey and can help the hundreds of millions of others who would benefit by this self knowledge of learning differently. According to 2019 U.S. Census Bureau, 20% of the United States (65.6 million people) have learning and attention issues. So you see, you and Mikey are not alone.

Mikey has gone through elementary, middle school, high school, and college. He had some difficulty but he used what he learned about how he learns differently and asked for help when he needed it. This allowed him to be stronger than ever expected, he even made the Dean's list in college and graduated with a Bachelor's Degree. Mikey now has 3 children who do not see him as having a disability, but just as a fun Dad.

Elementary School

Middle School

College

Fatherhood

Life is a never ending journey of learning. Throughout life, a learning disability doesn't force you to learn more or less than anyone else, but rather differently. Differences of all kinds should always be celebrated and embraced; it's a part of what makes us all unique. The world isn't meant to be uniformed robots that all think alike. It's meant to have everyone as free thinkers who all have a gift to think differently. Mikey went from being a student to a teacher and so can you.

If you have ever felt alone or broken, this book is written for you. Nothing about you is broken and there is nothing to fix. Throughout Mikey's life, he went from thinking a learning disability is a curse, to knowing it's a gift. The world thrives on diverse thinking. We are all wired differently. Above all, please know, you are not alone.

To order additional copies of this book, contact:
Xlibris
844-714-8691
www.Xlibris.com
Orders@Xlibris.com

ISBN: Softcover   978-1-6698-3693-3
         EBook   978-1-6698-3692-6

Print information available on the last page

Rev. date: 10/05/2022

Printed in the United States
by Baker & Taylor Publisher Services